10
minute

Spelling
Tests

for ages 8-9

Published 2009 by A & C Black Publishers Limited
36 Soho Square, London W1D 3QY
www.acblack.com

ISBN 9781408110836

Copyright © A & C Black Publishers Limited
Written by Andrew Brodie
Page layout by Bob Vickers

A CIP record for this publication is available from the British Library.

Printed in Great Britain by Martins the Printers, Berwick-upon-Tweed.

This book is produced using paper that is made from wood grown in managed, sustainable forests. It is natural, renewable and recyclable. The logging and manufacturing processes conform to the environmental regulations of the country of origin.

To see our full range of titles visit www.acblack.com

CONTENTS

Ten Minute Spelling Tests 8–9

This book will help all teachers to monitor and record their pupils' progress in spelling:

- 37 tests that are quick and easy to administer will allow you to gain evidence of pupils' achievement.
- Teachers' notes for each spelling test provide all focus words and the complete sentences to either dictate to the children or listen to on the accompanying audio CD.
- A recording grid on the CD enables you to assess and record individual children's progress

Ten Minute Spelling Tests and the National Strategies

The first two books in the series are designed for Key Stage 1 and closely follow the specifications of 'Letters and Sounds'.

The next four books, of which this is the second, build on the solid foundation from Key Stage 1 and provide systematic assessment of the Spelling Programme for Key Stage 2.

The spelling tests can be used as part of your programme of teaching spelling, fitting well into the sequence suggested for the National Strategies:

- Revise, explain, use
- Teach, model, define
- Practise, explore, investigate
- Apply, assess, reflect

The National Strategies suggest that spelling could be taught in five fifteen minute sessions over a two week period but that a flexible approach should be used to reflect the needs of the children. This resource would be well-suited to a process of teaching, defining, revising and investigating over two fifteen minute sessions then the ten minute assessment each week.

This book includes the medium frequency words to be taught in Year 4 and also features a range of words with particular spelling patterns or with specific prefixes and suffixes. You could use each set of words as your 'words of the week' for the children to practise ready for the test or you may choose to assess pupils' progress simply by administering each test and identifying gaps in knowledge.

What's on the CD

The accompanying CD contains:

- Audio files of each spelling test that can be used as an alternative to you dictating the sentences
- Printable and photocopiable PDFs of all the spelling tests
- A recording grid in which individual children's progress can be recorded. The recording grid enables you to copy the focus words from the grid into your planning and other activity sheets if you wish. Suggested method of recording: Leave the box empty if the child is unsuccessful. Select 'YES' if the child is confident with the sound, letter or word. Note that this record sheet covers lists of sounds and words for spelling from Phases Two to Six of Letters and Sounds so you can assess individual pupils against these lists before assessing them against the lists that appear in Ten Minute Spelling Tests for ages 8–9. Certain sounds and words that are common sources of error are repeated.

should

shouldn't

would

wouldn't

could

couldn't

can't

didn't

I'm

don't

Teachers' notes

This test provides assessment of some of the more common contractions and includes the medium frequency words didn't, can't, don't and I'm.

The words in the list on the left can be copied for children to take home to practise before they complete the assessment activity.

You can dictate the sentences below to the children but you may prefer to use the audio track on the CD – listening to a recording sometimes improves the children's concentration on the task. The sentences each feature one or more of the focus words – the sentences appear on the pupils' worksheet with the focus words missing. The sentence is read to the child for her/him to follow on the worksheet, noticing the missing word or words. The missing word is then repeated. You may need to pause the CD to allow the pupils time to write the word.

Here is the text that the children will hear on the audio CD:

Spelling Test 1

1	The teacher said I should work hard today.	should
2	She said I shouldn't talk too much.	shouldn't
3	I would like to go on holiday.	would
4	If I was on holiday I wouldn't have to do my spellings.	wouldn't
5	I wish I could fly all the way round the world.	could
6	My sister couldn't come with me.	couldn't
7	My brother can't come either.	can't
8	Yesterday I didn't have a spelling test.	didn't
9	When I'm older I won't have to practise spelling.	I'm

Listen carefully to sentence 10 then write the whole sentence. I will say the sentence twice.

10 I don't have any more spellings to do.

   I don't have any more spellings to do.

Andrew Brodie: Ten Minute Spelling Tests for ages 8–9 © A&C Black 2009

Name

Date

Listen to each sentence very carefully.
Write the missing word in each sentence.

1   The teacher said I _____ work hard today.

2   She said I _____ talk too much.

3   I _____ like to go on holiday.

4   If I was on holiday I _____ have to do my
      spellings.

5   I wish I _____ fly all the way round the world.

6   My sister _____ come with me.

7   My brother _____ come either.

8   Yesterday I _____ have a spelling test.

9   When _____ older I won't have to practise
      spelling.

Listen very carefully then write the whole sentence.

10   _____

      _____

go

going

gone

goes

went

come

coming

does

hear

heard

Teachers' notes

This test provides assessment of some of the more common root words that have irregular amendments for tense changes. The list includes the medium frequency words does, goes, gone, coming and heard.

The words in the list on the left can be copied for children to take home to practise before they complete the assessment activity.

You can dictate the sentences below to the children but you may prefer to use the audio track on the CD – listening to a recording sometimes improves the children's concentration on the task. The sentences each feature one or more of the focus words – the sentences appear on the pupils' worksheet with the focus words missing. The sentence is read to the child for her/him to follow on the worksheet, noticing the missing word or words. The missing word is then repeated. You may need to pause the CD to allow the pupils time to write the word.

Here is the text that the children will hear on the audio CD:

Spelling Test 2

1	The word go is very easy to spell.	go
2	I am going to play outside later if it's not raining.	going
3	Lots of people have gone to London today.	gone
4	The cat goes out at night to catch mice.	goes
5	Sometimes I go swimming but yesterday I went cycling instead.	went
6	"Do you want to come to my party?" my friend asked me.	come
7	"I'm coming too," said my other friend.	coming
8	The girl does really good paintings.	does
9	I can hear some people outside.	hear

Listen carefully to sentence 10 then write the whole sentence. I will say the sentence twice.

10   I heard a really good song yesterday but I can't remember how it goes.

     I heard a really good song yesterday but I can't remember how it goes.

Andrew Brodie: Ten Minute Spelling Tests for ages 8–9 © A&C Black 2009

Name

Date

Listen to each sentence very carefully.
Write the missing word in each sentence.

1   The word _____ is very easy to spell.

2   I am _____ to play outside later if it's not
     raining.

3   Lots of people have _____ to London today.

4   The cat _____ out at night to catch mice.

5   Sometimes I go swimming but yesterday I
     _____ cycling instead.

6   "Do you want to _____ to my party?"
     my friend asked me.

7   "I'm _____ too," said my other friend.

8   The girl _____ really good paintings.

9   I can _____ some people outside.

Listen very carefully then write the whole sentence.

10   _____

     _____

found

jumped

know

knew

leave

might

opened

show

started

tries

Teachers' notes

This test provides assessment of some common root words, some of which have irregular amendments for tense changes. You may wish to discuss the root words with the children, asking them for example to identify the root word related to 'found'. All of the words on the list are medium frequency words recommended for learning in Year 4. Note that sentence 10 contains some additional medium frequency words: brother, write and only.

The words in the list on the left can be copied for children to take home to practise before they complete the assessment activity.

You can dictate the sentences below to the children but you may prefer to use the audio track on the CD – listening to a recording sometimes improves the children's concentration on the task. The sentences each feature one or more of the focus words – the sentences appear on the pupils' worksheet with the focus words missing. The sentence is read to the child for her/him to follow on the worksheet, noticing the missing word or words. The missing word is then repeated. You may need to pause the CD to allow the pupils time to write the word.

Here is the text that the children will hear on the audio CD:

Spelling Test 3

1	We found the cat stuck up a tree.	found
2	The cat must have jumped up then couldn't get down again.	jumped
3	Do you know all of your multiplication tables?	know
4	Everybody knew that we had to practise our spellings.	knew
5	Shut the door quietly when you leave.	leave
6	The cat might get down without any help.	might
7	The door opened slowly, then the boy came in to the classroom.	opened
8	"Come and show me your work," said the teacher.	show
9	Everybody started work after that.	started

Listen carefully to sentence 10 then write the whole sentence. I will say the sentence twice.

10 My brother tries to write his own name but he's only four.

My brother tries to write his own name but he's only four.

Andrew Brodie: Ten Minute Spelling Tests for ages 8–9 © A&C Black 2009

Name

Date

Listen to each sentence very carefully.
Write the missing word in each sentence.

1   We _____ the cat stuck up a tree.

2   The cat must have _____ up then couldn't get
    down again.

3   Do you _____ all of your multiplication tables?

4   Everybody _____ that we had to practise our
    spellings.

5   Shut the door quietly when you _____.

6   The cat _____ get down without any help.

7   The door _____ slowly, then the boy came in to
    the classroom.

8   "Come and _____ me your work," said the
    teacher.

9   Everybody _____ work after that.

Listen very carefully then write the whole sentence.

10 _____

    _____

turn

turned

use

using

used

walk

walked

walking

woke

woken

Teachers' notes

This test provides assessment of some of the medium frequency words and the effects of changing tense.

The words in the list on the left can be copied for children to take home to practise before they complete the assessment activity.

You can dictate the sentences below to the children but you may prefer to use the audio track on the CD – listening to a recording sometimes improves the children's concentration on the task. The sentences each feature one or more of the focus words – the sentences appear on the pupils' worksheet with the focus words missing. The sentence is read to the child for her/him to follow on the worksheet, noticing the missing word or words. The missing word is then repeated. You may need to pause the CD to allow the pupils time to write the word.

Here is the text that the children will hear on the audio CD:

Spelling Test 4

1   When we play a game my sister always thinks
    it's her turn.   turn
2   Mum turned the pancake over by tossing it in the air.   turned
3   Can I use a pen to write my name?   use
4   I was using a new pencil but it kept breaking.   using
5   I made lots of blots on my paper when I used a pen.   used
6   Do you come to school in the car or do you walk?   walk
7   When we went on holiday we walked for miles.   walked
8   I prefer running to walking because it's faster.   walking
9   My brother woke me really early this morning.   woke

Listen carefully to sentence 10 then write the whole sentence.
I will say the sentence twice.

10   My brother was woken up by a dog barking.

     My brother was woken up by a dog barking.

Andrew Brodie: Ten Minute Spelling Tests for ages 8–9 © A&C Black 2009

Name

Date

Listen to each sentence very carefully.
Write the missing word in each sentence.

1   When we play a game my sister always thinks it's her
     _____.

2   Mum _____ the pancake over by tossing it
     in the air.

3   Can I _____ a pen to write my name?

4   I was _____ a new pencil but it kept breaking.

5   I made lots of blots on my paper when I _____
     a pen.

6   Do you come to school in the car or do you
     _____?

7   When we went on holiday we _____ for miles.

8   I prefer running to _____ because it's faster.

9   My brother _____ me really early this morning.

Listen very carefully then write the whole sentence.

10   _____

     _____

play

played

playing

stop

stopped

stopping

shopping

save

saved

saving

Teachers' notes

This test provides further assessment of changing tense. The test includes the medium frequency word stopped. You may like to point out the homophones bored and board.

The words in the list on the left can be copied for children to take home to practise before they complete the assessment activity.

You can dictate the sentences below to the children but you may prefer to use the audio track on the CD – listening to a recording sometimes improves the children's concentration on the task. The sentences each feature one or more of the focus words – the sentences appear on the pupils' worksheet with the focus words missing. The sentence is read to the child for her/him to follow on the worksheet, noticing the missing word or words. The missing word is then repeated. You may need to pause the CD to allow the pupils time to write the word.

Here is the text that the children will hear on the audio CD:

Spelling Test 5

1	If the weather is nice I like to play outside.	play
2	We were bored so we played a board game.	played
3	We were playing very well until my brother got cross.	playing
4	Mum told us to stop arguing.	stop
5	We stopped arguing but we also stopped talking to each other!	stopped
6	The rain is stopping so we can go outside.	stopping
7	On Saturday we went shopping.	shopping
8	If I save enough money I'm going to buy a bike.	save
9	Grace Darling was famous because she saved lots of people from drowning.	saved

Listen carefully to sentence 10 then write the whole sentence. I will say the sentence twice.

10 My mum is saving up for a new car.

My mum is saving up for a new car.

Name

Date

Listen to each sentence very carefully.
Write the missing word in each sentence.
Question 5 needs the same word twice.

1   If the weather is nice I like to _____ outside.

2   We were bored so we _____ a board game.

3   We were _____ very well until my brother got cross.

4   Mum told us to _____ arguing.

5   We _____ arguing but we also _____ talking to each other!

6   The rain is _____ so we can go outside.

7   On Saturday we went _____.

8   If I _____ enough money I'm going to buy a bike.

9   Grace Darling was famous because she _____ lots of people from drowning.

Listen very carefully then write the whole sentence.

10   _____

_____

change

changes

changed

changing

watch

watches

watched

ask

asking

asked

Teachers' notes

This test provides further assessment of changing tense. The test includes the medium frequency words change, watch, ask and asked.

The words in the list on the left can be copied for children to take home to practise before they complete the assessment activity.

You can dictate the sentences below to the children but you may prefer to use the audio track on the CD – listening to a recording sometimes improves the children's concentration on the task. The sentences each feature one or more of the focus words – the sentences appear on the pupils' worksheet with the focus words missing. The sentence is read to the child for her/him to follow on the worksheet, noticing the missing word or words. The missing word is then repeated. You may need to pause the CD to allow the pupils time to write the word.

Here is the text that the children will hear on the audio CD:

Spelling Test 6

1	When I grow up I am going to change the world.	change
2	My gran doesn't like changes.	changes
3	Our spelling list changed this week.	changed
4	There was a lot of water on the floor when we were changing for swimming.	changing
5	I don't watch much television because I prefer to play outside.	watch
6	My brother watches lots of television.	watches
7	I watched a very good programme yesterday.	watched
8	I had to ask for permission to go out.	ask
9	My little sister keeps asking Mum to pick her up.	asking

Listen carefully to sentence 10 then write the whole sentence. I will say the sentence twice.

10 My teacher asked me to change my book.

My teacher asked me to change my book.

Andrew Brodie: Ten Minute Spelling Tests for ages 8–9 © A&C Black 2009

Name

Date

Listen to each sentence very carefully.
Write the missing word in each sentence.

1   When I grow up I am going to _____ the world.

2   My gran doesn't like _____.

3   Our spelling list _____ this week.

4   There was a lot of water on the floor when we were
     _____ for swimming.

5   I don't _____ much television because I prefer
     to play outside.

6   My brother _____ lots of television.

7   I _____ a very good programme yesterday.

8   I had to _____ for permission to go out.

9   My little sister keeps _____ Mum to pick her up.

Listen very carefully then write the whole sentence.

10   _____

      _____

carry

carried

carrying

carries

carriage

marry

marries

marrying

married

marriage

Teachers' notes

This test provides further assessment of changing tense, in the context of word families from the root words carry and marry. The nouns carriage and marriage are also introduced.

The words in the list on the left can be copied for children to take home to practise before they complete the assessment activity.

You can dictate the sentences below to the children but you may prefer to use the audio track on the CD – listening to a recording sometimes improves the children's concentration on the task. The sentences each feature one or more of the focus words – the sentences appear on the pupils' worksheet with the focus words missing. The sentence is read to the child for her/him to follow on the worksheet, noticing the missing word or words. The missing word is then repeated. You may need to pause the CD to allow the pupils time to write the word.

Here is the text that the children will hear on the audio CD:

Spelling Test 7

1	My mum likes me to help carry the shopping.	carry
2	Last week I carried a chair home from a car boot sale and it was very heavy.	carried
3	I saw a bird carrying a big twig to make its nest.	carrying
4	An aeroplane carries people over long distances.	carries
5	We had a ride on a carriage pulled by a horse.	carriage
6	On the film the man asked the woman to marry him.	marry
7	The man marries the woman and the woman marries the man.	marries
8	I went to the ceremony when my cousin was marrying her fiance.	marrying
9	They got married last year.	married

Listen carefully to sentence 10 then write the whole sentence.
I will say the sentence twice.

10 After the marriage the man and woman rode in a carriage.

After the marriage the man and woman rode in a carriage.

Name _____   **Date** _____

Listen to each sentence very carefully.
Write the missing word in each sentence.

1   My mum likes me to help _____ the shopping.

2   Last week I _____ a chair home from a car
     boot sale and it was very heavy.

3   I saw a bird _____ a big twig to make its nest.

4   An aeroplane _____ people over long distances.

5   We had a ride on a _____ pulled by a horse.

6   On the film the man asked the woman to _____
     him.

7   The man _____ the woman and the woman
     _____ the man.

8   I went to the ceremony when my cousin was
     _____ her fiance.

9   They got _____ last year.

Listen very carefully then write the whole sentence.

10   _____

     _____

music

musical

magic

magical

fantastic

season

seasonal

tradition

traditional

hospital

Teachers' notes

This test provides an assessment focus for the word endings ic and al.

The words in the list on the left can be copied for children to take home to practise before they complete the assessment activity.

You can dictate the sentences below to the children but you may prefer to use the audio track on the CD – listening to a recording sometimes improves the children's concentration on the task. The sentences each feature one or more of the focus words – the sentences appear on the pupils' worksheet with the focus words missing. The sentence is read to the child for her/him to follow on the worksheet, noticing the missing word or words. The missing word is then repeated. You may need to pause the CD to allow the pupils time to write the word.

Here is the text that the children will hear on the audio CD:

Spelling Test 8

1   We hear lots of music every day at home, in school and in shops. music

2   My family went to see a musical show. musical

3   I thought the show was fantastic. fantastic

4   Some people believe in magic and some people don't. magic

5   The advert said that visiting the theme park was a magical experience. magical

6   Next season my favourite team are playing in the Premier League. season

7   In this country the weather is very seasonal. seasonal

8   It is a tradition to blow out candles on a birthday cake. tradition

9   A kilt is a traditional costume in Scotland. traditional

Listen carefully to sentence 10 then write the whole sentence. I will say the sentence twice.

10   The doctors and nurses in the hospital were fantastic.

The doctors and nurses in the hospital were fantastic.

Name

Date

Listen to each sentence very carefully.
Write the missing word in each sentence.

1   We hear lots of _____ every day at home, in school and in shops.

2   My family went to see a _____ show.

3   I thought the show was _____.

4   Some people believe in _____ and some people don't.

5   The advert said that visiting the theme park was a _____ experience.

6   Next _____ my favourite team are playing in the Premier League.

7   In this country the weather is very _____.

8   It is a _____ to blow out candles on a birthday cake.

9   A kilt is a _____ costume in Scotland.

Listen very carefully then write the whole sentence.

10   _____

_____

there

their

they're

night

knight

which

witch

stare

stair

too

Teachers' notes

This test provides assessment of some common homophones.

The words in the list on the left can be copied for children to take home to practise before they complete the assessment activity.

You can dictate the sentences below to the children but you may prefer to use the audio track on the CD – listening to a recording sometimes improves the children's concentration on the task. The sentences each feature one or more of the focus words – the sentences appear on the pupils' worksheet with the focus words missing. The sentence is read to the child for her/him to follow on the worksheet, noticing the missing word or words. The missing word is then repeated. You may need to pause the CD to allow the pupils time to write the word.

Here is the text that the children will hear on the audio CD:

Spelling Test 9

1	I liked Scotland when I went there on my holiday.	there
2	The people next door wash their car every weekend.	their
3	They're very fussy about keeping the car clean.	they're
4	Last night I couldn't get to sleep because I was so excited about my spelling test.	night
5	The knight wore armour and a helmet and he carried a shield.	knight
6	I don't know which way to spell some words.	which
7	In the story of Snow White the witch gave Snow White an apple.	witch
8	My mum says it's rude to stare at people.	stare
9	I like to sit on the third stair up from the bottom.	stair

Listen carefully to sentence 10 then write the whole sentence. I will say the sentence twice.

10   Mum says you shouldn't eat too many sweets but I only had two.

Mum says you shouldn't eat too many sweets but I only had two.

Andrew Brodie: Ten Minute Spelling Tests for ages 8–9 © A&C Black 2009

Name

Date

Listen to each sentence very carefully.
Write the missing word in each sentence.

1   I liked Scotland when I went _____ on my holiday.

2   The people next door wash _____ car every weekend.

3   _____ very fussy about keeping the car clean.

4   Last _____ I couldn't get to sleep because I was so excited about my spelling test.

5   The _____ wore armour and a helmet and he carried a shield.

6   I don't know _____ way to spell some words.

7   In the story of Snow White the _____ gave Snow White an apple.

8   My mum says it's rude to _____ at people.

9   I like to sit on the third _____ up from the bottom.

Listen very carefully then write the whole sentence.

10   _____

    _____

write

wrote

writing

written

buy

bought

bring

brought

tell

told

Teachers' notes

This test provides further assessment of changing tense, in the context of word families from the root words write, buy, bring and tell. The list includes the medium frequency words write, brought and told.

The words in the list on the left can be copied for children to take home to practise before they complete the assessment activity.

You can dictate the sentences below to the children but you may prefer to use the audio track on the CD – listening to a recording sometimes improves the children's concentration on the task. The sentences each feature one or more of the focus words – the sentences appear on the pupils' worksheet with the focus words missing. The sentence is read to the child for her/him to follow on the worksheet, noticing the missing word or words. The missing word is then repeated. You may need to pause the CD to allow the pupils time to write the word.

Here is the text that the children will hear on the audio CD:

Spelling Test 10

1   The teacher told us to write our spellings very carefully.   write

2   After my birthday I wrote a letter to my grandparents to thank them for my present.   wrote

3   I am writing very carefully.   writing

4   I have written lots of words since I have been in this class.   written

5   I try not to buy fizzy drinks because they can damage teeth.   buy

6   I bought a stamp to put on the envelope that I sent to my grandparents.   bought

7   "Bring your work to show me," said the teacher.   bring

8   Yesterday I brought my new football to school.   brought

9   Why did you tell me to get up early today?   tell

Listen carefully to sentence 10 then write the whole sentence. I will say the sentence twice.

10   The teacher told me that my writing is getting better.

The teacher told me that my writing is getting better.

Andrew Brodie: Ten Minute Spelling Tests for ages 8–9 © A&C Black 2009

Name

Date

Listen to each sentence very carefully.
Write the missing word in each sentence.

1   The teacher told us to _____ our spellings very carefully.

2   After my birthday I _____ a letter to my grandparents to thank them for my present.

3   I am _____ very carefully.

4   I have _____ lots of words since I have been in this class.

5   I try not to _____ fizzy drinks because they can damage teeth.

6   I _____ a stamp to put on the envelope that I sent to my grandparents.

7   "_____ your work to show me," said the teacher.

8   Yesterday I _____ my new football to school.

9   Why did you _____ me to get up early today?

Listen very carefully then write the whole sentence.

10   _____

_____

catch

caught

fight

fought

fly

flight

flew

wear

wore

worn

Teachers' notes

This test provides further assessment of changing tense, in the context of word families from the root words catch, fight, fly and wear.

The words in the list on the left can be copied for children to take home to practise before they complete the assessment activity.

You can dictate the sentences below to the children but you may prefer to use the audio track on the CD – listening to a recording sometimes improves the children's concentration on the task. The sentences each feature one or more of the focus words – the sentences appear on the pupils' worksheet with the focus words missing. The sentence is read to the child for her/him to follow on the worksheet, noticing the missing word or words. The missing word is then repeated. You may need to pause the CD to allow the pupils time to write the word.

Here is the text that the children will hear on the audio CD:

Spelling Test 11

1	I tried hard to catch the ball but I dropped it.	catch
2	The girl caught the ball brilliantly.	caught
3	When we were out for a walk our dog began to fight with another one.	fight
4	I read a story in which some children fought with pirates.	fought
5	Some birds can fly very high in the sky.	fly
6	A swift will sleep while it's in flight.	flight
7	A bird flew into our window but it was all right.	flew
8	Every day I wear my school uniform.	wear
9	When I went to a wedding I wore very smart clothes.	wore

Listen carefully to sentence 10 then write the whole sentence.
I will say the sentence twice.

10 I have worn these socks so much that I have made holes in them.

I have worn these socks so much that I have made holes in them.

Andrew Brodie: Ten Minute Spelling Tests for ages 8–9 © A&C Black 2009

Name _____ **Date** _____

Listen to each sentence very carefully.
Write the missing word in each sentence.

1   I tried hard to _____ the ball but I dropped it.

2   The girl _____ the ball brilliantly.

3   When we were out for a walk our dog began to
    _____ with another one.

4   I read a story in which some children _____
    with pirates.

5   Some birds can _____ very high in the sky.

6   A swift will sleep while it's in _____.

7   A bird _____ into our window but it was all right.

8   Every day I _____ my school uniform.

9   When I went to a wedding I _____ very smart
    clothes.

Listen very carefully then write the whole sentence.

10   _____

     _____

calf

calves

half

halves

himself

herself

themselves

knife

knives

loaves

Teachers' notes

This test provides assessment of the special case of changing some singular words containing the closing phoneme /f/ to plurals with the phoneme /v/.

The words in the list on the left can be copied for children to take home to practise before they complete the assessment activity.

You can dictate the sentences below to the children but you may prefer to use the audio track on the CD – listening to a recording sometimes improves the children's concentration on the task. The sentences each feature one or more of the focus words – the sentences appear on the pupils' worksheet with the focus words missing. The sentence is read to the child for her/him to follow on the worksheet, noticing the missing word or words. The missing word is then repeated. You may need to pause the CD to allow the pupils time to write the word.

Here is the text that the children will hear on the audio CD:

Spelling Test 12

1	The calf was following its mother across the field.	calf
2	There were seven calves in the field altogether.	calves
3	I ate half of my breakfast before getting changed.	half
4	Mum cut the pizzas into halves.	halves
5	My brother ate three whole pizzas himself.	himself
6	Mum didn't have any herself.	herself
7	Some people don't share, they keep everything for themselves.	themselves
8	You can cut pizzas with a knife or you can get a special pizza cutter.	knife
9	"Put the knives and forks on the table, please," said Mum.	knives

Listen carefully to sentence 10 then write the whole sentence. I will say the sentence twice.

10   We had three loaves of bread to share out.

   We had three loaves of bread to share out.

Name _____   **Date** _____

Listen to each sentence very carefully.
Write the missing word in each sentence.

1   The _____ was following its mother across
     the field.

2   There were seven _____ in the field altogether.

3   I ate _____ of my breakfast before getting
     changed.

4   Mum cut the pizzas into _____.

5   My brother ate three whole pizzas _____.

6   Mum didn't have any _____.

7   Some people don't share, they keep everything for
     _____.

8   You can cut pizzas with a _____ or you can
     get a special pizza cutter.

9   "Put the _____ and forks on the table, please,"
     said Mum.

Listen very carefully then write the whole sentence.

10   _____

     _____

fright

frighten

frightening

tight

tighten

tightening

height

freight

eight

straight

Teachers' notes

This test provides assessment of words with the letter string ight. Note that the letters igh give the phoneme /ie/, the letters eigh give the phoneme /ae/ except in the word height, and the letters aigh also give the phoneme /ae/.

The words in the list on the left can be copied for children to take home to practise before they complete the assessment activity.

You can dictate the sentences below to the children but you may prefer to use the audio track on the CD – listening to a recording sometimes improves the children's concentration on the task. The sentences each feature one or more of the focus words – the sentences appear on the pupils' worksheet with the focus words missing. The sentence is read to the child for her/him to follow on the worksheet, noticing the missing word or words. The missing word is then repeated. You may need to pause the CD to allow the pupils time to write the word.

Here is the text that the children will hear on the audio CD:

Spelling Test 13

1   I had a terrible fright when the door blew open.   fright
2   My brother tries to frighten me but he never does.   frighten
3   Some of the rides at the theme park were quite frightening.   frightening
4   My old shoes were tight because my feet had grown.   tight
5   I had to tighten my seat belt to make it fit.   tighten
6   The ropes on the tent needed tightening.   tightening
7   I am nearly the same height as my friend.   height
8   The train didn't carry passengers, it carried freight.   freight
9   Last year I was eight years old.   eight

Listen carefully to sentence 10 then write the whole sentence. I will say the sentence twice.

10   I was frightened by the dark so I ran straight home.
     I was frightened by the dark so I ran straight home.

Name

Date

Listen to each sentence very carefully.
Write the missing word in each sentence.

1 I had a terrible _____ when the door blew open.

2 My brother tries to _____ me but he never does.

3 Some of the rides at the theme park were quite

_____.

4 My old shoes were _____ because my feet had grown.

5 I had to _____ my seat belt to make it fit.

6 The ropes on the tent needed _____.

7 I am nearly the same _____ as my friend.

8 The train didn't carry passengers, it carried

_____.

9 Last year I was _____ years old.

Listen very carefully then write the whole sentence.

10 _____

_____

appointment

library

February

Wednesday

tomorrow

beautiful

because

began

being

before

Teachers' notes

This test provides assessment of a variety of useful words including the medium frequency words began and being and words such as February and library that are often spelt incorrectly.

The words in the list on the left can be copied for children to take home to practise before they complete the assessment activity.

You can dictate the sentences below to the children but you may prefer to use the audio track on the CD – listening to a recording sometimes improves the children's concentration on the task. The sentences each feature one or more of the focus words – the sentences appear on the pupils' worksheet with the focus words missing. The sentence is read to the child for her/him to follow on the worksheet, noticing the missing word or words. The missing word is then repeated. You may need to pause the CD to allow the pupils time to write the word.

Here is the text that the children will hear on the audio CD:

Spelling Test 14

1	I had an appointment to see the doctor.	appointment
2	I went to the library but it was closed.	library
3	February has fewer days than the other months.	February
4	Wednesday is in the middle of the school week.	Wednesday
5	I am going to have my hair cut the day after tomorrow.	tomorrow
6	Mum says that her hair looks beautiful.	beautiful
7	I like the weekend because we do fun things.	because
8	Our day out began badly as the train was late.	began
9	It's not much fun being indoors on a sunny day.	being

Listen carefully to sentence 10 then write the whole sentence. I will say the sentence twice.

10 The day before tomorrow is today.

The day before tomorrow is today.

Andrew Brodie: Ten Minute Spelling Tests for ages 8–9 © A&C Black 2009

Name

Date

Listen to each sentence very carefully.
Write the missing word in each sentence.

1   I had an _____ to see the doctor.

2   I went to the _____ but it was closed.

3   _____ has fewer days than the other months.

4   _____ is in the middle of the school week.

5   I am going to have my hair cut the day after
_____.

6   Mum says that her hair looks _____.

7   I like the weekend _____ we do fun things.

8   Our day out _____ badly as the train was late.

9   It's not much fun _____ indoors on a sunny day.

Listen very carefully then write the whole sentence.

10   _____

_____

apology

apologise

length

lengthen

educate

education

able

ability

stupid

stupidity

Teachers' notes

This test provides assessment of a variety of some common suffixes that may change the endings of the root words. You may wish to ask the children which of the root words has not been changed by the addition of a suffix.

The words in the list on the left can be copied for children to take home to practise before they complete the assessment activity.

You can dictate the sentences below to the children but you may prefer to use the audio track on the CD – listening to a recording sometimes improves the children's concentration on the task. The sentences each feature one or more of the focus words – the sentences appear on the pupils' worksheet with the focus words missing. The sentence is read to the child for her/him to follow on the worksheet, noticing the missing word or words. The missing word is then repeated. You may need to pause the CD to allow the pupils time to write the word.

Here is the text that the children will hear on the audio CD:

Spelling Test 15

1 After I had an argument I had to give an apology to the other person.   apology

2 If you have done something wrong you should admit it and apologise.   apologise

3 "Look at the length of my trousers," I said to my mum.   length

4 "We may need to buy some new ones unless I can lengthen them," she said.   lengthen

5 Teachers work hard in schools to educate their pupils.   educate

6 We are lucky to have a good education.   education

7 Are you able to help other people?   able

8 I wish I had the ability to score more goals.   ability

9 Sometimes everybody makes stupid mistakes.   stupid

Listen carefully to sentence 10 then write the whole sentence. I will say the sentence twice.

10 The teacher told the boy off for his stupidity.

The teacher told the boy off for his stupidity.

Andrew Brodie: Ten Minute Spelling Tests for ages 8–9 © A&C Black 2009

Name

Date

Listen to each sentence very carefully.
Write the missing word in each sentence.

1 After I had an argument I had to give an
_____ to the other person.

2 If you have done something wrong you should admit it
and _____.

3 "Look at the _____ of my trousers," I said to
my mum.

4 "We may need to buy some new ones unless I can
_____ them," she said.

5 Teachers work hard in schools to _____ their
pupils.

6 We are lucky to have a good _____.

7 Are you _____ to help other people?

8 I wish I had the _____ to score more goals.

9 Sometimes everybody makes _____ mistakes.

Listen very carefully then write the whole sentence.

10 _____

_____

sadness	
silliness	
drowsiness	
darkness	
softness	
agreement	
enjoyment	
entertainment	
government	
parliament	

Teachers' notes

This test provides assessment of words that contain the suffixes ness or ment. Do the children know to remove the y from silly to create silliness?

The words in the list on the left can be copied for children to take home to practise before they complete the assessment activity.

You can dictate the sentences below to the children but you may prefer to use the audio track on the CD – listening to a recording sometimes improves the children's concentration on the task. The sentences each feature one or more of the focus words – the sentences appear on the pupils' worksheet with the focus words missing. The sentence is read to the child for her/him to follow on the worksheet, noticing the missing word or words. The missing word is then repeated. You may need to pause the CD to allow the pupils time to write the word.

Here is the text that the children will hear on the audio CD:

Spelling Test 16

1	Happiness is much better than sadness.	sadness
2	"I don't want any more silliness," said the teacher.	silliness
3	As soon as the teacher mentioned spellings a feeling of drowsiness came over me.	drowsiness
4	My eyes had to adjust to the darkness when the lights went out.	darkness
5	Babies like the softness of their cuddly toys.	softness
6	I made an agreement to go to bed on time.	agreement
7	Everybody felt the same enjoyment of the show.	enjoyment
8	The comedian provided great entertainment with his jokes.	entertainment
9	The government makes decisions for all the people.	government

Listen carefully to sentence 10 then write the whole sentence. I will say the sentence twice.

10 The government meets in the Houses of Parliament.

The government meets in the Houses of Parliament.

Andrew Brodie: Ten Minute Spelling Tests for ages 8–9 © A&C Black 2009

Name

Date

Listen to each sentence very carefully.
Write the missing word in each sentence.

1   Happiness is much better than _____.

2   "I don't want any more _____," said the teacher.

3   As soon as the teacher mentioned spellings a feeling of
_____ came over me.

4   My eyes had to adjust to the _____ when the
lights went out.

5   Babies like the _____ of their cuddly toys.

6   I made an _____ to go to bed on time.

7   Everybody felt the same _____ of the show.

8   The comedian provided great _____ with his
jokes.

9   The _____ makes decisions for all the people.

Listen very carefully then write the whole sentence.

10   _____

_____

neighbour

neighbourhood

childhood

friendship

membership

relationship

partnership

workmanship

championship

ownership

Teachers' notes

This test provides assessment of words that contain the suffixes hood and ship, giving the opportunity to practise some useful root words.

The words in the list on the left can be copied for children to take home to practise before they complete the assessment activity.

You can dictate the sentences below to the children but you may prefer to use the audio track on the CD – listening to a recording sometimes improves the children's concentration on the task. The sentences each feature one or more of the focus words – the sentences appear on the pupils' worksheet with the focus words missing. The sentence is read to the child for her/him to follow on the worksheet, noticing the missing word or words. The missing word is then repeated. You may need to pause the CD to allow the pupils time to write the word.

Here is the text that the children will hear on the audio CD:

Spelling Test 17

1	I don't see my next door neighbour very often.	neighbour
2	Most people in our neighbourhood are quite friendly.	neighbourhood
3	It is important to enjoy childhood.	childhood
4	I am lucky to have a great friendship with my best friend.	friendship
5	My mum was given membership of a swimming club.	membership
6	The instructor has a good relationship with the members.	relationship
7	The school has a partnership with the secondary school.	partnership
8	Most builders are proud of their workmanship.	workmanship
9	I think the best team won the championship.	championship

Listen carefully to sentence 10 then write the whole sentence. I will say the sentence twice.

10   John was given ownership of the boat.

John was given ownership of the boat.

Andrew Brodie: Ten Minute Spelling Tests for ages 8–9 © A&C Black 2009

Name _____

Date _____

Listen to each sentence very carefully.
Write the missing word in each sentence.

1   I don't see my next door _____ very often.

2   Most people in our _____ are quite friendly.

3   It is important to enjoy _____.

4   I am lucky to have a great _____ with my best friend.

5   My mum was given _____ of a swimming club.

6   The instructor has a good _____ with the members.

7   The school has a _____ with the secondary school.

8   Most builders are proud of their _____.

9   I think the best team won the _____.

Listen very carefully then write the whole sentence.

10 _____

    _____

any

every

much

never

often

only

still

until

upon

while

Teachers' notes

This test provides assessment of medium frequency words recommended for Term 2 of Year 4.

The words in the list on the left can be copied for children to take home to practise before they complete the assessment activity.

You can dictate the sentences below to the children but you may prefer to use the audio track on the CD – listening to a recording sometimes improves the children's concentration on the task. The sentences each feature one or more of the focus words – the sentences appear on the pupils' worksheet with the focus words missing. The sentence is read to the child for her/him to follow on the worksheet, noticing the missing word or words. The missing word is then repeated. You may need to pause the CD to allow the pupils time to write the word.

Here is the text that the children will hear on the audio CD:

Spelling Test 18

1 "Do you have any idea what you are doing?" asked the man crossly.   any

2 I try to get some exercise every day.   every

3 I don't have very much money in my pocket.   much

4 My dog never does what he's told.   never

5 I go swimming quite often.   often

6 Penguins only live naturally in the southern hemisphere.   only

7 I am still writing my spellings.   still

8 We don't go out to break until we have done our work.   until

9 Lots of fairy stories start with the words 'once upon a time'.   upon

Listen carefully to sentence 10 then write the whole sentence. I will say the sentence twice.

10 Every day we work while some people are asleep.

Every day we work while some people are asleep.

Andrew Brodie: Ten Minute Spelling Tests for ages 8–9 © A&C Black 2009

Name

Date

Listen to each sentence very carefully.
Write the missing word in each sentence.

1   "Do you have _____ idea what you are doing?" asked the man crossly.

2   I try to get some exercise _____ day.

3   I don't have very _____ money in my pocket.

4   My dog _____ does what he's told.

5   I go swimming quite _____.

6   Penguins _____ live naturally in the southern hemisphere.

7   I am _____ writing my spellings.

8   We don't go out to break _____ we have done our work.

9   Lots of fairy stories start with the words 'once _____ a time'.

Listen very carefully then write the whole sentence.

10   _____

      _____

bubble

kettle

common

suddenly

coffee

follow

swimming

cotton

butter

better

Teachers' notes

This test provides assessment of words that feature double consonants and includes the medium frequency words suddenly and better.

The words in the list on the left can be copied for children to take home to practise before they complete the assessment activity.

You can dictate the sentences below to the children but you may prefer to use the audio track on the CD – listening to a recording sometimes improves the children's concentration on the task. The sentences each feature one or more of the focus words – the sentences appear on the pupils' worksheet with the focus words missing. The sentence is read to the child for her/him to follow on the worksheet, noticing the missing word or words. The missing word is then repeated. You may need to pause the CD to allow the pupils time to write the word.

Here is the text that the children will hear on the audio CD:

Spelling Test 19

1   A large bubble appeared in the air.   bubble
2   Polly, put the kettle on please.   kettle
3   Swallows are quite common in the summer but
    in the winter they have gone.   common
4   Suddenly the girl disappeared down a rabbit hole.   suddenly
5   Does your teacher drink coffee or tea at break time?   coffee
6   "Would you please follow me," said the tour guide.   follow
7   Next week we are going swimming.   swimming
8   Did you know that cotton grows on bushes?   cotton
9   Do you like butter on your bread?   butter

Listen carefully to sentence 10 then write the whole sentence.
I will say the sentence twice.

10 Is bread better with butter or is butter better with bread?

    Is bread better with butter or is butter better with bread?

Name

Date

Listen to each sentence very carefully.
Write the missing word in each sentence.

1   A large _____ appeared in the air.

2   Polly, put the _____ on please.

3   Swallows are quite _____ in the summer but in
     the winter they have gone.

4   _____ the girl disappeared down a rabbit hole.

5   Does your teacher drink _____ or tea at break
     time?

6   "Would you please _____ me," said the tour
     guide.

7   Next week we are going _____.

8   Did you know that _____ grows on bushes?

9   Do you like _____ on your bread?

Listen very carefully then write the whole sentence.

10   _____

     _____

outside

sometimes

without

birthday

cupboard

fireplace

footwear

another

somewhere

indoors

Teachers' notes

This test provides assessment of compound words, including the medium frequency words sometimes, outside and without.

The words in the list on the left can be copied for children to take home to practise before they complete the assessment activity.

You can dictate the sentences below to the children but you may prefer to use the audio track on the CD – listening to a recording sometimes improves the children's concentration on the task. The sentences each feature one or more of the focus words – the sentences appear on the pupils' worksheet with the focus words missing. The sentence is read to the child for her/him to follow on the worksheet, noticing the missing word or words. The missing word is then repeated. You may need to pause the CD to allow the pupils time to write the word.

Here is the text that the children will hear on the audio CD:

Spelling Test 20

1   When the weather is good it's nice to be outside.   outside

2   Today I walked to school but I come in the car
    sometimes.   sometimes

3   I have my cereals without any sugar on them.   without

4   In what month is your birthday?   birthday

5   Put the paper away in the cupboard please.   cupboard

6   We don't have a fireplace in our house.   fireplace

7   Boots, shoes, sandals and flip-flops are different types
    of footwear.   footwear

8   "Would you like another sandwich?" asked Mum
    politely.   another

9   "I've put my keys down somewhere and now I can't
    find them," said the man.   somewhere

Listen carefully to sentence 10 then write the whole sentence.
I will say the sentence twice.

10   The cat stays indoors when it's raining.

     The cat stays indoors when it's raining.

  Andrew Brodie: Ten Minute Spelling Tests for ages 8–9 © A&C Black 2009

Name _____ **Date** _____

Listen to each sentence very carefully.
Write the missing word in each sentence.

1   When the weather is good it's nice to be _____.

2   Today I walked to school but I come in the car _____.

3   I have my cereals _____ any sugar on them.

4   In what month is your _____?

5   Put the paper away in the _____ please.

6   We don't have a _____ in our house.

7   Boots, shoes, sandals and flip-flops are different types of _____.

8   "Would you like _____ sandwich?" asked Mum politely.

9   "I've put my keys down _____ and now I can't find them," said the man.

Listen very carefully then write the whole sentence.

10   _____

_____

station

competition

question

information

subtraction

serious

obvious

precious

delicious

national

Teachers' notes

This test provides assessment of words ending with tion, ious or cious. Pupils should notice that the letter i makes the phoneme /ee/ in the words serious and obvious but not in any of the other words in the list.

The words in the list on the left can be copied for children to take home to practise before they complete the assessment activity.

You can dictate the sentences below to the children but you may prefer to use the audio track on the CD – listening to a recording sometimes improves the children's concentration on the task. The sentences each feature one or more of the focus words – the sentences appear on the pupils' worksheet with the focus words missing. The sentence is read to the child for her/him to follow on the worksheet, noticing the missing word or words. The missing word is then repeated. You may need to pause the CD to allow the pupils time to write the word.

Here is the text that the children will hear on the audio CD:

Spelling Test 21

1   We were rather late when we got to the station so we missed the train. station

2   Lots of people took part in the singing competition.   competition
3   The test was easy but I got stuck on the last question.   question
4   The teacher asked us to find information about
    World War Two.   information
5   Addition is easy but subtraction can be difficult
    sometimes.   subtraction
6   "I need to ask you a serious question," said the teacher.   serious
7   Sometimes the answer to a question is obvious.   obvious
8   Gold and platinum are precious metals.   precious
9   My mum makes delicious cakes.   delicious

Listen carefully to sentence 10 then write the whole sentence.
I will say the sentence twice.

10   He plays football for the national team.

     He plays football for the national team.

Andrew Brodie: Ten Minute Spelling Tests for ages 8–9 © A&C Black 2009

Name

Date

47

Listen to each sentence very carefully.
Write the missing word in each sentence.

1   We were rather late when we got to the
    _____ so we missed the train.

2   Lots of people took part in the singing _____.

3   The test was easy but I got stuck on the last
    _____.

4   The teacher asked us to find _____ about
    World War Two.

5   Addition is easy but _____ can be difficult
    sometimes.

6   "I need to ask you a _____ question," said the
    teacher.

7   Sometimes the answer to a question is _____.

8   Gold and platinum are _____ metals.

9   My mum makes _____ cakes.

Listen very carefully then write the whole sentence.

10   _____

    _____

through

enough

think

thought

cough

rough

ought

daughter

taught

laugh

Teachers' notes

This test provides assessment of words containing ough or augh. The list includes the word think so that a comparison can be made to its past tense, thought, which is a medium frequency word. Through is also a medium frequency word. Note that there are phonetic differences between words that contain the same letter strings, eg the ough makes different phonemes in the words through, enough, thought and cough.

The words in the list on the left can be copied for children to take home to practise before they complete the assessment activity.

You can dictate the sentences below to the children but you may prefer to use the audio track on the CD – listening to a recording sometimes improves the children's concentration on the task. The sentences each feature one or more of the focus words – the sentences appear on the pupils' worksheet with the focus words missing. The sentence is read to the child for her/him to follow on the worksheet, noticing the missing word or words. The missing word is then repeated. You may need to pause the CD to allow the pupils time to write the word.

Here is the text that the children will hear on the audio CD:

Spelling Test 22

1	The naughty boy threw a ball through the window.	through
2	"Have you had enough to eat?" asked Mum.	enough
3	I think multiplication is difficult.	think
4	I thought multiplication was difficult until I practised it and now I know it's easy.	thought
5	When you have a cold you sometimes develop a cough.	cough
6	The teacher told us to write a rough copy first, then to copy it in best handwriting.	rough
7	People aren't always nice to each other but they ought to be.	ought
8	My uncle has two sons and one daughter.	daughter
9	The teacher taught us our six times table.	taught

Listen carefully to sentence 10 then write the whole sentence. I will say the sentence twice.

10 Good jokes always make me laugh.

Good jokes always make me laugh.

Name

Date

49

Listen to each sentence very carefully.
Write the missing word in each sentence.

1   The naughty boy threw a ball _____ the window.

2   "Have you had _____ to eat?" asked Mum.

3   I _____ multiplication is difficult.

4   I _____ multiplication was difficult until I
      practised it and now I know it's easy.

5   When you have a cold you sometimes develop a
      _____.

6   The teacher told us to write a _____ copy first,
      then to copy it in best handwriting.

7   People aren't always nice to each other but they
      _____ to be.

8   My uncle has two sons and one _____.

9   The teacher _____ us our six times table.

Listen very carefully then write the whole sentence.

10   _____

       _____

always

also

already

altogether

although

alcove

round

around

along

almost

Teachers' notes

This test provides assessment of words featuring the prefix al or a – the word along has the prefix a rather than al. The list includes the medium frequency words almost, always, along, also and around.

The words in the list on the left can be copied for children to take home to practise before they complete the assessment activity.

You can dictate the sentences below to the children but you may prefer to use the audio track on the CD – listening to a recording sometimes improves the children's concentration on the task. The sentences each feature one or more of the focus words – the sentences appear on the pupils' worksheet with the focus words missing. The sentence is read to the child for her/him to follow on the worksheet, noticing the missing word or words. The missing word is then repeated. You may need to pause the CD to allow the pupils time to write the word.

Here is the text that the children will hear on the audio CD:

Spelling Test 23

1   People always enjoy being by the sea when the weather is good. — always

2   When you go swimming you need to take your swimming costume and you also need a towel. — also

3   You probably know most of your multiplication tables already. — already

4   There are three dogs and two cats altogether. — altogether

5   I stayed up late although I was very tired. — although

6   The treasure was hidden in a little alcove behind the old wardrobe. — alcove

7   We went there the long way round. — round

8   Our best friends live just around the corner from our house. — around

9   We had to sing along with the man playing the guitar. — along

Listen carefully to sentence 10 then write the whole sentence. I will say the sentence twice.

10   We are almost at the end of the test already.

We are almost at the end of the test already.

Name

Date

Listen to each sentence very carefully.
Write the missing word in each sentence.

1   People _____ enjoy being by the sea when the weather is good.

2   When you go swimming you need to take your swimming costume and you _____ need a towel.

3   You probably know most of your multiplication tables _____.

4   There are three dogs and two cats _____.

5   I stayed up late _____ I was very tired.

6   The treasure was hidden in a little _____ behind the old wardrobe.

7   We went there the long way _____.

8   Our best friends live just _____ the corner from our house.

9   We had to sing _____ with the man playing the guitar.

Listen very carefully then write the whole sentence.

10   _____

_____

first

second

third

fourth

fifth

sixth

seventh

eighth

ninth

tenth

Teachers' notes

This test provides assessment of ordinal numbers and includes the medium frequency words first and second.

The words in the list on the left can be copied for children to take home to practise before they complete the assessment activity.

You can dictate the sentences below to the children but you may prefer to use the audio track on the CD – listening to a recording sometimes improves the children's concentration on the task. The sentences each feature one or more of the focus words – the sentences appear on the pupils' worksheet with the focus words missing. The sentence is read to the child for her/him to follow on the worksheet, noticing the missing word or words. The missing word is then repeated. You may need to pause the CD to allow the pupils time to write the word.

Here is the text that the children will hear on the audio CD:

Spelling Test 24

1   January is the first month of the year.   first
2   The second day of the school week is Tuesday.   second
3   We shared the cake so I had a third of it.   third
4   The fourth month of the year is April.   fourth
5   My brother's birthday is on the fifth of August.   fifth
6   The sixth performer on the show was a singer.   sixth
7   I came seventh in the swimming race.   seventh
8   The eighth month of the year is August.   eighth
9   Do you know what the ninth month of the year is?   ninth

Listen carefully to sentence 10 then write the whole sentence. I will say the sentence twice.

10 One tenth of a hundred is ten.

One tenth of a hundred is ten.

Name _____   **Date** _____

Listen to each sentence very carefully.
Write the missing word in each sentence.

1   January is the _____ month of the year.

2   The _____ day of the school week is Tuesday.

3   We shared the cake so I had a _____ of it.

4   The _____ month of the year is April.

5   My brother's birthday is on the _____ of August.

6   The _____ performer on the show was a singer.

7   I came _____ in the swimming race.

8   The _____ month of the year is August.

9   Do you know what the _____ month of the year is?

Listen very carefully then write the whole sentence.

10   _____

     _____

four

fourteen

forty

young

double

trouble

journey

sound

route

pound

Teachers' notes

This test provides assessment of words containing ou, with the notable exception of the word forty – it is useful to contrast this word with the words four, fourteen and fourth. The list includes the medium frequency word young.

The words in the list on the left can be copied for children to take home to practise before they complete the assessment activity.

You can dictate the sentences below to the children but you may prefer to use the audio track on the CD – listening to a recording sometimes improves the children's concentration on the task. The sentences each feature one or more of the focus words – the sentences appear on the pupils' worksheet with the focus words missing. The sentence is read to the child for her/him to follow on the worksheet, noticing the missing word or words. The missing word is then repeated. You may need to pause the CD to allow the pupils time to write the word.

Here is the text that the children will hear on the audio CD:

Spelling Test 25

1	My little sister is four years old.	four
2	My big brother is fourteen years old.	fourteen
3	It's a very long time until I will be forty years old.	forty
4	Sometimes I'm not allowed to do things because I'm too young.	young
5	One hundred is double fifty.	double
6	It's best to try to keep out of trouble.	trouble
7	From this country to Australia is a very long journey.	journey
8	"When I go out of the room I don't want to hear a sound," said the teacher.	sound
9	What route does the plane take to get to Australia?	route

Listen carefully to sentence 10 then write the whole sentence. I will say the sentence twice.

10 Each drink cost more than a pound and I needed to buy four of them.

Each drink cost more than a pound and I needed to buy four of them.

Name

Date

Listen to each sentence very carefully.
Write the missing word in each sentence.

1   My little sister is _____ years old.

2   My big brother is _____ years old.

3   It's a very long time until I will be _____ years old.

4   Sometimes I'm not allowed to do things because I'm too _____.

5   One hundred is _____ fifty.

6   It's best to try to keep out of _____.

7   From this country to Australia is a very long _____.

8   "When I go out of the room I don't want to hear a _____," said the teacher.

9   What _____ does the plane take to get to Australia?

Listen very carefully then write the whole sentence.

10   _____

_____

metre

centimetre

millimetre

kilometre

litre

millilitre

gram

kilogram

length

number

Teachers' notes

This test provides assessment of words related to measurement – note that the test features the plural versions of many of the words. The list includes the medium frequency word number.

The words in the list on the left can be copied for children to take home to practise before they complete the assessment activity.

You can dictate the sentences below to the children but you may prefer to use the audio track on the CD – listening to a recording sometimes improves the children's concentration on the task. The sentences each feature one or more of the focus words – the sentences appear on the pupils' worksheet with the focus words missing. The sentence is read to the child for her/him to follow on the worksheet, noticing the missing word or words. The missing word is then repeated. You may need to pause the CD to allow the pupils time to write the word.

Here is the text that the children will hear on the audio CD:

Spelling Test 26

1   I am over one metre tall.   metre
2   There are one hundred centimetres in a metre.   centimetres
3   There are one thousand millimetres in a metre.   millimetres
4   One thousand metres make a kilometre.   kilometre
5   Liquids can be measured in litres.   litres
6   There are one thousand millilitres in one litre.   millilitres
7   A gram is a very small unit for measuring mass.   gram
8   One thousand grams make a kilogram.   kilogram
9   When you weigh yourself what number do the
    scales show?   number

Listen carefully to sentence 10 then write the whole sentence.
I will say the sentence twice.

10   Millimetres, centimetres, metres and kilometres are all units of length.

     Millimetres, centimetres, metres and kilometres are all units of length.

Andrew Brodie: Ten Minute Spelling Tests for ages 8–9 © A&C Black 2009

Name

Date

Listen to each sentence very carefully.
Write the missing word in each sentence.

1   I am over one _____ tall.

2   There are one hundred _____ in a metre.

3   There are one thousand _____ in a metre.

4   One thousand metres make a _____.

5   Liquids can be measured in _____.

6   There are one thousand _____ in one litre.

7   A _____ is a very small unit for measuring mass.

8   One thousand grams make a _____.

9   When you weigh yourself what _____ do the scales show?

Listen very carefully then write the whole sentence.

10   _____

_____

Andrew Brodie: Ten Minute Spelling Tests for ages 8–9 © A&C Black 2009

hour

minute

second

week

during

month

year

before

morning

today

Teachers' notes

This test provides assessment of words related to time. The list includes the medium frequency words second, before, during, morning, today and year.

The words in the list on the left can be copied for children to take home to practise before they complete the assessment activity.

You can dictate the sentences below to the children but you may prefer to use the audio track on the CD – listening to a recording sometimes improves the children's concentration on the task. The sentences each feature one or more of the focus words – the sentences appear on the pupils' worksheet with the focus words missing. The sentence is read to the child for her/him to follow on the worksheet, noticing the missing word or words. The missing word is then repeated. You may need to pause the CD to allow the pupils time to write the word.

Here is the text that the children will hear on the audio CD:

Spelling Test 27

1	Lunch time lasts for one hour in some schools.	hour
2	The spelling test takes about ten minutes.	minutes
3	Each question could take about thirty seconds.	seconds
4	Most classes have their spelling test at the end of the week.	week
5	You should listen carefully during the spelling test.	during
6	My birthday is in the month of January.	month
7	Next year I will be in a new class.	year
8	I went to the dentist's the day before yesterday.	before
9	I woke up very early this morning.	morning

Listen carefully to sentence 10 then write the whole sentence.
I will say the sentence twice.

10 Before I left home today I brushed my teeth for two minutes.

Before I left home today I brushed my teeth for two minutes.

Name

Date

Listen to each sentence very carefully.
Write the missing word in each sentence.

1   Lunch time lasts for one _____ in some schools.

2   The spelling test takes about ten _____.

3   Each question could take about thirty _____.

4   Most classes have their spelling test at the end of the

_____.

5   You should listen carefully _____ the spelling test.

6   My birthday is in the _____ of January.

7   Next _____ I will be in a new class.

8   I went to the dentist's the day _____ yesterday.

9   I woke up very early this _____.

Listen very carefully then write the whole sentence.

10   _____

_____

active

forgive

massive

expense

expensive

relations

relatives

compete

competition

competitive

Teachers' notes

This test provides assessment of words containing the letter string ive, together with related words. Note that we have used the words relations and relatives as synonyms – you may like to ask the pupils to create sentences using these words in other ways.

The words in the list on the left can be copied for children to take home to practise before they complete the assessment activity.

You can dictate the sentences below to the children but you may prefer to use the audio track on the CD – listening to a recording sometimes improves the children's concentration on the task. The sentences each feature one or more of the focus words – the sentences appear on the pupils' worksheet with the focus words missing. The sentence is read to the child for her/him to follow on the worksheet, noticing the missing word or words. The missing word is then repeated. You may need to pause the CD to allow the pupils time to write the word.

Here is the text that the children will hear on the audio CD:

Spelling Test 28

1   It is important to take exercise and keep active.   active

2   When people are sorry you should forgive them for
     their mistakes.   forgive

3   The old oak tree was massive.   massive

4   Going on holiday often creates a lot of expense.   expense

5   The ice cream was very tasty but it was also
     very expensive.   expensive

6   I have lots of friends and relations.   relations

7   My relatives live all over the world.   relatives

8   I would like to compete in a talent show.   compete

9   We had a competition to see who was best at
     balancing.   competition

Listen carefully to sentence 10 then write the whole sentence.
I will say the sentence twice.

10 Most of my relatives are very competitive.

     Most of my relatives are very competitive.

Andrew Brodie: Ten Minute Spelling Tests for ages 8–9 © A&C Black 2009

Name

Date

Listen to each sentence very carefully.
Write the missing word in each sentence.

1   It is important to take exercise and keep _____.

2   When people are sorry you should _____ them
    for their mistakes.

3   The old oak tree was _____.

4   Going on holiday often creates a lot of _____.

5   The ice cream was very tasty but it was also very
    _____.

6   I have lots of friends and _____.

7   My _____ live all over the world.

8   I would like to _____ in a talent show.

9   We had a _____ to see who was best at
    balancing.

Listen very carefully then write the whole sentence.

10   _____

     _____

river

diver

hover

hovercraft

above

favourite

flavour

leave

television

develop

Teachers' notes

This test provides assessment of words containing the letter v and includes the medium frequency word above.

The words in the list on the left can be copied for children to take home to practise before they complete the assessment activity.

You can dictate the sentences below to the children but you may prefer to use the audio track on the CD – listening to a recording sometimes improves the children's concentration on the task. The sentences each feature one or more of the focus words – the sentences appear on the pupils' worksheet with the focus words missing. The sentence is read to the child for her/him to follow on the worksheet, noticing the missing word or words. The missing word is then repeated. You may need to pause the CD to allow the pupils time to write the word.

Here is the text that the children will hear on the audio CD:

Spelling Test 29

1 It's nice to walk along by the river but make sure you don't fall in.   river

2 The diver found treasure when he swam down to the old wreck.   diver

3 The kestrel is a bird that can hover in the air while it looks for prey.   hover

4 A hovercraft can move over land or water.   hovercraft

5 In my house my bedroom is above the kitchen.   above

6 My favourite colour is green.   favourite

7 I think the best flavour of ice cream is vanilla.   flavour

8 We had to leave early so that we could catch our bus. leave

9 I would like to appear on television.   television

Listen carefully to sentence 10 then write the whole sentence. I will say the sentence twice.

10 I would like to develop my skills in all ball games.

I would like to develop my skills in all ball games.

Name

Date

Listen to each sentence very carefully.
Write the missing word in each sentence.

1   It's nice to walk along by the _____ but make
    sure you don't fall in.

2   The _____ found treasure when he swam
    down to the old wreck.

3   The kestrel is a bird that can _____ in the air
    while it looks for prey.

4   A _____ can move over land or water.

5   In my house my bedroom is _____ the kitchen.

6   My _____ colour is green.

7   I think the best _____ of ice cream is vanilla.

8   We had to _____ early so that we could catch
    our bus.

9   I would like to appear on _____.

Listen very carefully then write the whole sentence.

10   _____

     _____

both

following

high

near

other

place

right

such

through

together

This test provides assessment of medium frequency words recommended for teaching in Term 3 of Year 4.

The words in the list on the left can be copied for children to take home to practise before they complete the assessment activity.

You can dictate the sentences below to the children but you may prefer to use the audio track on the CD – listening to a recording sometimes improves the children's concentration on the task. The sentences each feature one or more of the focus words – the sentences appear on the pupils' worksheet with the focus words missing. The sentence is read to the child for her/him to follow on the worksheet, noticing the missing word or words. The missing word is then repeated. You may need to pause the CD to allow the pupils time to write the word.

Here is the text that the children will hear on the audio CD:

Spelling Test 30

1	My brother and I both like playing football.	both
2	Not next year but the following year I will be in Year Six.	following
3	The flag is flying high above the castle.	high
4	There are lots of shops near to where I live.	near
5	"Pass me the other plates," said Mum.	other
6	The beach is a very good place for a picnic when the weather is good.	place
7	My mum says that I don't know my left from right!	right
8	When we were on holiday we had such good weather that we spent every day on the beach.	such
9	If you enter the house through the front door the stairs are straight ahead.	through

Listen carefully to sentence 10 then write the whole sentence. I will say the sentence twice.

10 My friends and I like to go to places together.

My friends and I like to go to places together.

Name

Date

Listen to each sentence very carefully.
Write the missing word in each sentence.

1   My brother and I _____ like playing football.

2   Not next year but the _____ year I will be in
     Year Six.

3   The flag is flying _____ above the castle.

4   There are lots of shops _____ to where I live.

5   "Pass me the _____ plates," said Mum.

6   The beach is a very good _____ for a picnic
     when the weather is good.

7   My mum says that I don't know my left from
     _____!

8   When we were on holiday we had _____
     good weather that we spent every day on the beach.

9   If you enter the house _____ the front door
     the stairs are straight ahead.

Listen very carefully then write the whole sentence.

10   _____

      _____

break

broke

broken

pack

package

rocket

ticket

sticker

sprinkle

wrinkled

Teachers' notes

This test provides assessment of words containing the letter k.

The words in the list on the left can be copied for children to take home to practise before they complete the assessment activity.

You can dictate the sentences below to the children but you may prefer to use the audio track on the CD – listening to a recording sometimes improves the children's concentration on the task. The sentences each feature one or more of the focus words – the sentences appear on the pupils' worksheet with the focus words missing. The sentence is read to the child for her/him to follow on the worksheet, noticing the missing word or words. The missing word is then repeated. You may need to pause the CD to allow the pupils time to write the word.

Here is the text that the children will hear on the audio CD:

Spelling Test 31

1 Don't break the eggs when you carry them home. break

2 When we got home we found that two of the eggs had broken. broken

3 We had to have the car repaired when it broke down. broke

4 "Make sure you pack your swimming bag ready for tomorrow," said Mum. pack

5 The postman delivered a big package to our house. package

6 The best firework was a great big rocket. rocket

7 After I got on the train I couldn't find my ticket. ticket

8 When I went to the dentist I was given a sticker for cleaning my teeth well. sticker

9 My mum likes to sprinkle chocolate powder on her coffee. sprinkle

Listen carefully to sentence 10 then write the whole sentence. I will say the sentence twice.

10 The package was wrinkled and broken.

    The package was wrinkled and broken.

Name

Date

Listen to each sentence very carefully.
Write the missing word in each sentence.

1   Don't _____ the eggs when you carry them home.

2   When we got home we found that two of the eggs had
     _____ .

3   We had to have the car repaired when it _____
     down.

4   "Make sure you _____ your swimming bag
     ready for tomorrow," said Mum.

5   The postman delivered a big _____ to our house.

6   The best firework was a great big _____ .

7   After I got on the train I couldn't find my _____ .

8   When I went to the dentist I was given a _____
     for cleaning my teeth well.

9   My mum likes to _____ chocolate powder on
     her coffee.

Listen very carefully then write the whole sentence.

10   _____

     _____

water

wander

wonder

wonderful

wallow

woman

women

word

world

ward

Teachers' notes

This test provides assessment of words beginning with w. The word water is a high frequency word but it is frequently spelt incorrectly.

The words in the list on the left can be copied for children to take home to practise before they complete the assessment activity.

You can dictate the sentences below to the children but you may prefer to use the audio track on the CD – listening to a recording sometimes improves the children's concentration on the task. The sentences each feature one or more of the focus words – the sentences appear on the pupils' worksheet with the focus words missing. The sentence is read to the child for her/him to follow on the worksheet, noticing the missing word or words. The missing word is then repeated. You may need to pause the CD to allow the pupils time to write the word.

Here is the text that the children will hear on the audio CD:

Spelling Test 32

1	The water in the pool was lovely and warm.	water
2	Mum made us wander around all the shops.	wander
3	Sometimes I wonder why we have to go shopping.	wonder
4	The hippopotamus likes to wallow in mud.	wallow
5	A woman on the train was talking loudly on her phone.	woman
6	Lots of men and women run in the marathon.	women
7	"I'd like a word with you," said the teacher crossly.	word
8	All over the world people are working hard to save the environment.	world
9	When I was in hospital I was in a ward with lots of friendly people.	ward

Listen carefully to sentence 10 then write the whole sentence. I will say the sentence twice.

10 When we were in Wales the weather was wonderful.

When we were in Wales the weather was wonderful.

Andrew Brodie: Ten Minute Spelling Tests for ages 8–9 © A&C Black 2009

Name

Date

Listen to each sentence very carefully.
Write the missing word in each sentence.

1   The _____ in the pool was lovely and warm.

2   Mum made us _____ around all the shops.

3   Sometimes I _____ why we have to go shopping.

4   The hippopotamus likes to _____ in mud.

5   A _____ on the train was talking loudly on her
     phone.

6   Lots of men and _____ run in the marathon.

7   "I'd like a _____ with you," said the teacher
     crossly.

8   All over the _____ people are working hard to
     save the environment.

9   When I was in hospital I was in a _____ with
     lots of friendly people.

Listen very carefully then write the whole sentence.

10   _____

     _____

nice

rice

spice

dice

twice

mice

police

notice

icicle

icy

Teachers' notes

This test provides assessment of words containing the letter string ice together with the related words icy and icicle.

The words in the list on the left can be copied for children to take home to practise before they complete the assessment activity.

You can dictate the sentences below to the children but you may prefer to use the audio track on the CD – listening to a recording sometimes improves the children's concentration on the task. The sentences each feature one or more of the focus words – the sentences appear on the pupils' worksheet with the focus words missing. The sentence is read to the child for her/him to follow on the worksheet, noticing the missing word or words. The missing word is then repeated. You may need to pause the CD to allow the pupils time to write the word.

Here is the text that the children will hear on the audio CD:

Spelling Test 33

1 The teacher said we should be nice and quiet. nice
2 One of my favourite meals is curry with rice. rice
3 Curry is made with hot spices. spices
4 To see who should go first we all rolled dice. dice
5 It wasn't fair because my brother had twice as many presents as me. twice
6 The farmer's wife chased three blind mice. mice
7 When I was lost at the shops the police helped me. police
8 You should take no notice when people call you names. notice
9 It was so cold that an icicle formed from the dripping tap. icicle

Listen carefully to sentence 10 then write the whole sentence. I will say the sentence twice.

10 The weather is nice when it's icy.

The weather is nice when it's icy.

Name

Date

Listen to each sentence very carefully.
Write the missing word in each sentence.

1   The teacher said we should be _____ and quiet.

2   One of my favourite meals is curry with _____.

3   Curry is made with hot _____.

4   To see who should go first we all rolled _____.

5   It wasn't fair because my brother had _____ as many presents as me.

6   The farmer's wife chased three blind _____.

7   When I was lost at the shops the _____ helped me.

8   You should take no _____ when people call you names.

9   It was so cold that an _____ formed from the dripping tap.

Listen very carefully then write the whole sentence.

10   _____

_____

difficult

difficulty

difference

different

differently

easy

easily

easier

similar

similarity

Teachers' notes

This test provides assessment of words that make comparisons. The list includes the medium frequency word different.

The words in the list on the left can be copied for children to take home to practise before they complete the assessment activity.

You can dictate the sentences below to the children but you may prefer to use the audio track on the CD – listening to a recording sometimes improves the children's concentration on the task. The sentences each feature one or more of the focus words – the sentences appear on the pupils' worksheet with the focus words missing. The sentence is read to the child for her/him to follow on the worksheet, noticing the missing word or words. The missing word is then repeated. You may need to pause the CD to allow the pupils time to write the word.

Here is the text that the children will hear on the audio CD:

Spelling Test 34

1	Some words are difficult to spell.	difficult
2	Other words are easy to spell.	easy
3	I sometimes have difficulty with spelling long words.	difficulty
4	The twins are so alike some people can't tell the difference between them.	difference
5	Because I know them well I can see that they are quite different to each other.	different
6	Sometimes they dress the same but usually they are differently dressed.	differently
7	I go to sleep very easily but it's hard to wake up again.	easily
8	Some people think maths is easier than spelling.	easier
9	My friend and I like similar things.	similar

Listen carefully to sentence 10 then write the whole sentence.
I will say the sentence twice.

10 There's a lot of similarity between cats and dogs but in some ways they are quite different.

There's a lot of similarity between cats and dogs but in some ways they are quite different.

Andrew Brodie: Ten Minute Spelling Tests for ages 8–9 © A&C Black 2009

Name

Date

Listen to each sentence very carefully.
Write the missing word in each sentence.

1   Some words are _____ to spell.

2   Other words are _____ to spell.

3   I sometimes have _____ with spelling long words.

4   The twins are so alike some people can't tell the
    _____ between them.

5   Because I know them well I can see that they are quite
    _____ to each other.

6   Sometimes they dress the same but usually they are
    _____ dressed.

7   I go to sleep very _____ but it's hard to wake
    up again.

8   Some people think maths is _____ than spelling.

9   My friend and I like _____ things.

Listen very carefully then write the whole sentence.

10 _____

    _____

sudden

suddenly

second

secondly

hope

hoping

hopeful

hopefully

wonderful

wonderfully

Teachers' notes

This test provides assessment of adding suffixes to root words. The list includes the medium frequency words second and suddenly, both of which have been practised previously.

The words in the list on the left can be copied for children to take home to practise before they complete the assessment activity.

You can dictate the sentences below to the children but you may prefer to use the audio track on the CD – listening to a recording sometimes improves the children's concentration on the task. The sentences each feature one or more of the focus words – the sentences appear on the pupils' worksheet with the focus words missing. The sentence is read to the child for her/him to follow on the worksheet, noticing the missing word or words. The missing word is then repeated. You may need to pause the CD to allow the pupils time to write the word.

Here is the text that the children will hear on the audio CD:

Spelling Test 35

1   Everybody jumped when there was a sudden clap of thunder.   sudden

2   Suddenly it began to pour with rain.   suddenly

3   The second thing we had to do was to swim across the pool.   second

4   "Firstly, let me introduce myself then secondly let me introduce my owl," said the man.   secondly

5   "I hope that you enjoy the show," said the head teacher to the parents.   hope

6   I am hoping to get lots of presents on my birthday.   hoping

7   The teacher is hopeful of good results in the test.   hopeful

8   Hopefully I will get a good score.   hopefully

9   The show was absolutely wonderful.   wonderful

Listen carefully to sentence 10 then write the whole sentence. I will say the sentence twice.

10   The owl flew across the hall wonderfully.

The owl flew across the hall wonderfully.

Andrew Brodie: Ten Minute Spelling Tests for ages 8–9 © A&C Black 2009

Name

Date

Listen to each sentence very carefully.
Write the missing word in each sentence.

1   Everybody jumped when there was a _____
     clap of thunder.

2   _____ it began to pour with rain.

3   The _____ thing we had to do was to swim
     across the pool.

4   "Firstly, let me introduce myself then _____ let
     me introduce my owl," said the man.

5   "I _____ that you enjoy the show," said the
     head teacher to the parents.

6   I am _____ to get lots of presents on my birthday.

7   The teacher is _____ of good results in the test.

8   _____ I will get a good score.

9   The show was absolutely _____.

Listen very carefully then write the whole sentence.

10   _____

     _____

above

below

inside

where

under

across

over

behind

between

next

Teachers' notes

This test provides assessment of position words and includes the medium frequency words above, below, inside, where, under, across and between, some of which have been practised previously. You may like to ask the pupils which of the words has been used in a sentence related to time rather than to position.

The words in the list on the left can be copied for children to take home to practise before they complete the assessment activity.

You can dictate the sentences below to the children but you may prefer to use the audio track on the CD – listening to a recording sometimes improves the children's concentration on the task. The sentences each feature one or more of the focus words – the sentences appear on the pupils' worksheet with the focus words missing. The sentence is read to the child for her/him to follow on the worksheet, noticing the missing word or words. The missing word is then repeated. You may need to pause the CD to allow the pupils time to write the word.

Here is the text that the children will hear on the audio CD:

Spelling Test 36

1	The helicopter hovered above the cliff.	above
2	The injured girl was on a ledge just below the top of the cliff.	below
3	It's better to stay inside when it's raining outdoors.	inside
4	"Do you know where to go?" asked the secretary.	where
5	The pound coin rolled under the chair.	under
6	We took it in turns to go across the rope bridge.	across
7	When the match was over everybody went home.	over
8	It was easy to find the boy because he hid behind the curtain.	behind
9	The sweet shop is between the newsagents and the bank.	between

Listen carefully to sentence 10 then write the whole sentence. I will say the sentence twice.

10   The joke book is on the next shelf above the poetry books.

The joke book is on the next shelf above the poetry books.

Name

Date

Listen to each sentence very carefully.
Write the missing word in each sentence.

1   The helicopter hovered _____ the cliff.

2   The injured girl was on a ledge just _____ the top of the cliff.

3   It's better to stay _____ when it's raining outdoors.

4   "Do you know _____ to go?" asked the secretary.

5   The pound coin rolled _____ the chair.

6   We took it in turns to go _____ the rope bridge.

7   When the match was _____ everybody went home.

8   It was easy to find the boy because he hid _____ the curtain.

9   The sweet shop is _____ the newsagents and the bank.

Listen very carefully then write the whole sentence.

10   _____

_____

possible

impossible

terrible

horrible

responsible

enjoyable

valuable

breakable

drinkable

miserable

Teachers' notes

This test provides assessment of words ending with ible or able.

The words in the list on the left can be copied for children to take home to practise before they complete the assessment activity.

You can dictate the sentences below to the children but you may prefer to use the audio track on the CD – listening to a recording sometimes improves the children's concentration on the task. The sentences each feature one or more of the focus words – the sentences appear on the pupils' worksheet with the focus words missing. The sentence is read to the child for her/him to follow on the worksheet, noticing the missing word or words. The missing word is then repeated. You may need to pause the CD to allow the pupils time to write the word.

Here is the text that the children will hear on the audio CD:

Spelling Test 37

1 "Is it possible to buy stamps here?" the man asked.   possible

2 I think it's impossible to swim across the
   Atlantic Ocean.   impossible

3 The weather was so terrible that three boats sank.   terrible

4 "Try not to be horrible to each other," my mum
   told us.   horrible

5 "You will need to behave in a responsible way
   on this trip," said the teacher.   responsible

6 The trip was the most enjoyable one we have ever had.   enjoyable

7 "Don't break this, it's very valuable," said the man
   as he gave me the jug.   valuable

8 Jugs, plates and dishes are easily breakable.   breakable

9 Some water is too dirty to be drinkable.   drinkable

Listen carefully to sentence 10 then write the whole sentence.
I will say the sentence twice.

10 When you have had an enjoyable day you don't feel miserable.

    When you have had an enjoyable day you don't feel miserable.

     Andrew Brodie: Ten Minute Spelling Tests for ages 8–9 © A&C Black 2009

Name

Date

Listen to each sentence very carefully.
Write the missing word in each sentence.

1   "Is it _____ to buy stamps here?" the man asked.

2   I think it's _____ to swim across the Atlantic
Ocean.

3   The weather was so _____ that three boats sank.

4   "Try not to be _____ to each other," my mum
told us.

5   "You will need to behave in a _____ way on
this trip," said the teacher.

6   The trip was the most _____ one we have
ever had.

7   "Don't break this, it's very _____," said the man
as he gave me the jug.

8   Jugs, plates and dishes are easily _____.

9   Some water is too dirty to be _____.

Listen very carefully then write the whole sentence.

10   _____

_____

RECORD SHEET

Child's name _____

Class _____

Date _____

should ☐ shouldn't ☐ would ☐ wouldn't ☐ could ☐ couldn't ☐ can't ☐ didn't ☐ I'm ☐ don't ☐

go ☐ going ☐ gone ☐ goes ☐ went ☐ come ☐ coming ☐ does ☐ hear ☐ heard ☐

found ☐ jumped ☐ know ☐ knew ☐ leave ☐ might ☐ opened ☐ show ☐ started ☐ tries ☐

turn ☐ turned ☐ use ☐ using ☐ used ☐ walk ☐ walked ☐ walking ☐ wake ☐ woke ☐ woken ☐

play ☐ played ☐ playing ☐ stop ☐ stopped ☐ stopping ☐ shopping ☐ save ☐ saved ☐ saving ☐

change ☐ changes ☐ changed ☐ changing ☐ watch ☐ watches ☐ watched ☐ ask ☐ asking ☐ asked ☐

carry ☐ carried ☐ carrying ☐ carries ☐ carriage ☐ marry ☐ marries ☐ marrying ☐ married ☐ marriage ☐

music ☐ musical ☐ magic ☐ magical ☐ fantastic ☐ season ☐ seasonal ☐ tradition ☐ traditional ☐ hospital ☐

there ☐ their ☐ they're ☐ night ☐ knight ☐ which ☐ witch ☐ stare ☐ stair ☐ too ☐

write ☐ wrote ☐ writing ☐ written ☐ buy ☐ bought ☐ bring ☐ brought ☐ tell ☐ told ☐

catch ☐ caught ☐ fight ☐ fought ☐ fly ☐ flight ☐ flew ☐ wear ☐ wore ☐ worn ☐

calf ☐ calves ☐ half ☐ halves ☐ himself ☐ herself ☐ themselves ☐ knife ☐ knives ☐ loaves ☐

fright ☐ frighten ☐ frightening ☐ tight ☐ tighten ☐ tightening ☐ height ☐ freight ☐ eight ☐ straight ☐

appointment ☐ library ☐ February ☐ Wednesday ☐ tomorrow ☐ beautiful ☐ because ☐ began ☐ being ☐ before ☐

apology ☐ apologise ☐ length ☐ lengthen ☐ educate ☐ education ☐ able ☐ ability ☐ stupid ☐ stupidity ☐

sadness ☐ silliness ☐ drowsiness ☐ darkness ☐ softness ☐ agreement ☐ enjoyment ☐ entertainment ☐ government ☐
parliament ☐

neighbour ☐ neighbourhood ☐ childhood ☐ friendship ☐ membership ☐ relationship ☐ partnership ☐ workmanship ☐
championship ☐ ownership ☐

any ☐ every ☐ much ☐ never ☐ often ☐ only ☐ still ☐ until ☐ upon ☐ while ☐

bubble ☐ kettle ☐ common ☐ suddenly ☐ coffee ☐ follow ☐ swimming ☐ cotton ☐ butter ☐ better ☐

outside ☐ sometimes ☐ without ☐ birthday ☐ cupboard ☐ fireplace ☐ footwear ☐ another ☐ somewhere ☐ indoors ☐

station ☐ competition ☐ question ☐ information ☐ subtraction ☐ serious ☐ obvious ☐ precious ☐ delicious ☐ national ☐

through ☐ enough ☐ think ☐ thought ☐ cough ☐ rough ☐ ought ☐ daughter ☐ taught ☐ laugh ☐

always ☐ also ☐ already ☐ altogether ☐ although ☐ alcove ☐ round ☐ around ☐ along ☐ almost ☐

first ☐ second ☐ third ☐ fourth ☐ fifth ☐ sixth ☐ seventh ☐ eighth ☐ ninth ☐ tenth ☐

four ☐ fourteen ☐ forty ☐ young ☐ double ☐ trouble ☐ journey ☐ sound ☐ route ☐ pound ☐

metre ☐ centimetre ☐ millimetre ☐ kilometre ☐ litre ☐ millilitre ☐ gram ☐ kilogram ☐ length ☐ number ☐

hour ☐ minute ☐ second ☐ week ☐ during ☐ month ☐ year ☐ before ☐ morning ☐ today ☐

active ☐ forgive ☐ massive ☐ expense ☐ expensive ☐ relation ☐ relative ☐ compete ☐ competition ☐ competitive ☐

river ☐ diver ☐ hover ☐ hovercraft ☐ above ☐ favourite ☐ flavour ☐ leave ☐ television ☐ develop ☐

both ☐ following ☐ high ☐ near ☐ other ☐ place ☐ right ☐ such ☐ through ☐ together ☐

break ☐ broke ☐ broken ☐ pack ☐ package ☐ rocket ☐ ticket ☐ sticker ☐ sprinkle ☐ wrinkled ☐

water ☐ wander ☐ wonder ☐ wonderful ☐ wallow ☐ woman ☐ women ☐ word ☐ world ☐ ward ☐

nice ☐ rice ☐ spice ☐ dice ☐ twice ☐ mice ☐ police ☐ notice ☐ icicle ☐ icy ☐

difficult ☐ difficulty ☐ difference ☐ different ☐ differently ☐ easy ☐ easily ☐ easier ☐ similar ☐ similarity ☐

sudden ☐ suddenly ☐ second ☐ secondly ☐ hope ☐ hoping ☐ hopeful ☐ hopefully ☐ wonderful ☐ wonderfully ☐

above ☐ below ☐ inside ☐ where ☐ under ☐ across ☐ over ☐ behind ☐ between ☐ next ☐

possible ☐ impossible ☐ terrible ☐ horrible ☐ responsible ☐ enjoyable ☐ valuable ☐ breakable ☐ drinkable ☐ miserable ☐

Andrew Brodie: Ten Minute Spelling Tests for ages 8–9 © A&C Black 2009